Conversation Starters

for

Emily St. John Mandel's

Station Eleven

By dailyBooks

FREE Download: Bonus Books Included
*Claim Yours with **Any Purchase** of* Conversation Starters!

  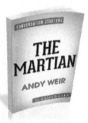

How to claim your free download:

1.   LEAVE MY AMAZON REVIEW.
You Can Also Use the "Write a Customer Review" Button

2.   ENTER YOUR BEST EMAIL HERE.
NO SPAM. Your Email is Never Shared and is Protected

Or Scan QR Code

3.   RECEIVE YOUR FREE DOWNLOAD.
Download is Delivered Instantly to Inbox

Tips for Using dailyBooks Conversation Starters:

EVERY GOOD BOOK CONTAINS A WORLD FAR DEEPER THAN the surface of its pages. The characters and their world come alive through the words on the pages, yet the characters and its world still live on. Questions herein are designed to bring us beneath the surface of the page and invite us into the world that lives on. These questions can be used to:

- Foster a deeper understanding of the book
- Promote an atmosphere of discussion for groups
- Assist in the study of the book, either individually or corporately
- Explore unseen realms of the book as never seen before

About Us:

THROUGH YEARS OF EXPERIENCE AND FIELD EXPERTISE, from newspaper featured book clubs to local library chapters, *dailyBooks* can bring your book discussion to life. Host your book party as we discuss some of today's most widely read books.

Table of Contents

Introducing *Station Eleven*
Introducing the Author

question 1
question 2
question 3
question 4
question 5
question 6
question 7
question 8
question 9
question 10
question 11
question 12
question 13
question 14
question 15
question 16
question 17
question 18
question 19
question 20
question 21
question 22
question 23
question 24
question 25
question 26
question 27
question 28
question 29
question 30
question 31
question 32

[question 33](question%2033)
[question 34](question%2034)
[question 35](question%2035)
[question 36](question%2036)
[question 37](question%2037)
[question 38](question%2038)
[question 39](question%2039)
[question 40](question%2040)
[question 41](question%2041)
[question 42](question%2042)
[question 43](question%2043)
[question 44](question%2044)
[question 45](question%2045)
[question 46](question%2046)
[question 47](question%2047)
[question 48](question%2048)
[question 49](question%2049)
[question 50](question%2050)

Introducing *Station Eleven*

STATION ELEVEN IS ONE OF THE MOST MAGNIFICENT mystery novels written by Emily St. Johns. The appalling beginning explains the sudden death of a renowned actor, Arthur Leander. He dies on the spot while performing as *King Lear* on stage. His death is witnessed by a young girl named Kristen, who is also performing in that play. The tragic death of the people's favorite actor happened on the same day as the dreadful Georgia flu breaks out in Toronto. This devastating flu not only ends the entire civilization but also leaves very few traces of life in the city.

Twenty years later, Kristen, one of the very few survivors, joins a traveling symphony of artists and musicians who travel around the world. Emily St. Johns has an edge in explaining the series of events before and after the flu outbreak. The novel has an extensive cast of characters, equally blended in the two shades of the story. Arthur Leander, being one of the major characters of the novel, had four wives, but his martial life remains very intricate. Apart from Arthur, Jeevan, an entertainment journalist, is his friend who tries to give him CPR, but to no avail and he doesn't survive.

Jeevan is also aware of various secrets associated with Arthur that are hidden from others.

Emily is spectacular in unfolding the ephemeral life of a celebrity—its limelight and how it ends in reality. The novel contains references, inspiration, and quotes from the famous Shakespeare plays. A significant part of the novel explains the journey of traveling symphony musicians moving to different places for their performances. They carry instruments, costumes, and luggage with them. Kristen, after the calamity, now enjoys her life as a member of the troupe.

The major twist in the story comes when some of the troupe gets separated from the rest and reaches St. Deborah in search of old civilizations. They encounter a person who calls himself a prophet who has some strong connectivity with their past. The flashback of Arthur's life also relates with the prophet and his followers. He seems like a serious threat to their lives once again.

Station Eleven explores a new perspective on human life, the materiality of the world, and art with splendid depth.

Introducing the Author

EMILY ST. JOHN MANDEL IS A CANADIAN NOVELIST famous for her enthralling writing. Born in 1979, Mandel studied contemporary dance at the School of Toronto Dance Theatre. She lived in Montreal for a short period and later on, she moved to New York.

Mandel has written three novels including the *Last Night in Montreal*, *The Singer's Gun*, and *the Lola Quartet* in the category of thriller fiction. While her fourth novel *Station Eleven*, published in 2014, was a huge hit, it brought enormous fame, recognition, and several awards to her. Unlike the other three novels, *Station Eleven* is a post-apocalyptic novel. Mandel has also written various short fiction stories and essays including the *Best American Mystery Stories* in 2013.

Mandel is an enthusiastic storyteller who possesses an inimitable style of blending mystery with thrill and terror. She is good at creating suspense and placing clues that give rise to thought provoking questions in the mind of the reader.

In *Station Eleven*, Mandel used the third-person style of narration. The narration is simple, yet it explains each and every character in detail. Her novels generally contain a wide range of characters. Each character has an individual plotline, which enables a strong grip on the novel throughout. The flashback of events before and after the catastrophic flu disaster is nicely interlinked. She has remarkably used the famous literature by William Shakespeare. She successfully relates the old civilizations with the modern state of technology. *Station Eleven* is her only novel that falls into the category of science fiction. The novel has been translated into 27 languages.

Through her novels, Mandel always tries to convey a message of peace, love, and human survival and creates space in the readers' minds to develop a thoughtful perspective. After winning the National Book Award for her fourth novel, *Station Eleven*, Mandel suggested other writers not rush after winning awards; instead, they should focus on their skills to come up with pioneering because awards and recognition come inevitably.

Discussion Questions

. . . .

question 1

Kristen Raymonde, a young girl, has witnessed Arthur's death while
performing on the stage. How do you think Arthur's death would have
affected Kristen?

. . . .

question 2

Jeevan, a paramedic in training, tried to give CPR to Arthur, but it was too late. What steps should he have taken to save Arthur's life?

. . . .

question 3

"Survival is insufficient," a famous line from *Star Trek,* is the motto of the traveling symphony. What do you think this statement means?

. . . .

. . . .

question 4

Twenty years after the flu outbreak, Kristen decides to travel with the traveling symphony. What do you think of her decision? What changes will this decision bring in Kristen's life?

. . . .

. . . .

question 5

When Kristen was interviewed about her memories twenty years after the disaster, she couldn't exactly remember. Why do you think that is?

. . . .

. . . .

question 6

The novel has an extensive range of characters. Who do you think the main
protagonist is and why?

. . . .

. . . .

question 7

The prophet says about death, "I'm not speaking of the tedious variations on physical death. There's the death of the body, and there's the death of the soul. I saw my mother die twice." In your opinion who was prophet's mother? What were the causes of her death?

. . . .

. . . .

question 8

Arthur's first wife, Miranda, was the author of *Station Eleven* comic books. What connectivity with the happenings of the story does that comic book have?

. . . .

question 9

The novel contains inspirations from famous plays by William Shakespeare.
How well does the concept of *Station Eleven* relate with those of
Shakespeare?

· ·

question 10

Frank, Jeevan's brother, had abdominal paralysis. He commits suicide during the flu outbreak. Why do you think he chose to commit suicide?

question 11

Arthur quotes from William Butler Yeats, "Love is like the lion's tooth."
What does that mean, and why is it on his mind?

question 12

The ending of the novel mentions Clarke Thompson. Who was Clarke? What trouble did he face after the collapse of civilization?

. . . .

question 13

Tyler Leander, the son of Arthur and his second wife Elizabeth, grows up as
a prophet. What do you think makes him a religious leader?

. . . .

. . . .

question 14

The novel powerfully connects the two time frames before and after the collapse of civilization. What message do you think Mandel tried to convey with the storyline?

. . . .

question 15

Arthur's death happens on the same night the Georgia flu arrived. What connects these two events?

question 16

Lindsay's Library and Bookish Comforts gave a 5-star rating to *Station Eleven*. Do you think this rating is justified? How would you rate this novel and why?

. . . .

question 17

Station Eleven won the Arthur C. Clarke Award and the Toronto Book
Award. Why do you think *Station Eleven* has enjoyed such success?

. . . .

. . . .

question 18

The Seattle Times believes that *Station Eleven* is haunting and hard to put down. Do you agree with this review? Why or why not?

. . . .

. . . .

question 19

Entertainment Weekly believes that the novel is a page-turner and poem. Why do you think the reviewer called it a poem?

. . . .

. . . .

question 20

The Washington Post defines this novel as "a surprisingly beautiful story of human relationships amid devastation." What do you think about human relationships and its factors for devastation?

. . . .

FREE Download: Bonus Books Included
*Claim Yours with **Any Purchase** of* Conversation Starters!

  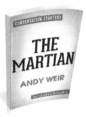

How to claim your free download:

4. **LEAVE MY AMAZON REVIEW.**
You Can Also Use "Write a Customer Review" Button

5. **ENTER YOUR BEST EMAIL HERE.**
NO SPAM. Your Email is Never Shared and is Protected

Or Scan Above

6. **RECEIVE YOUR FREE DOWNLOAD.**
Download is Instantly Delivered to Inbox

question 21

Station Eleven has been included in the *Washington Post*'s list of Ten Best Books of the Year. Do you think this book is deserving of such high praise? Why or why not?

. . . .

question 22

The *New York Times* Book Review believes that "*Station Eleven* is as much a
mystery as it is a post-apocalyptic tale." Do you agree with this review?
What is your opinion on the mystery of this novel?

. . . .

question 23

Bustle believes that this novel is strange, poetic, thrilling, and grim all at the same time. Did you feel all these factors while reading? Discuss how they worked together in the story.

. . . .

question 24

Sarah McCarry remarked this novel as "a big, brilliant, ambitious, genre-bending novel." In your opinion which factors distinguish this novel from other novels?

. . . .

question 25

Los Angeles Review of Books thinks that terror and empathy were both impressively displayed by Emily Mandel. Which terror part of the novel impressed you and why?

. . . .

question 26

The *New York Times* remarked that Mandel is an able and exuberant storyteller. Do you agree with the statement? What quality of Emily Mandel impresses you and why?

. . . .

. . . .

question 27

Mandel has an omniscient style of narrative writing. What aspects does she often cover in her stories?

. . . .

. . . .

question 28

Mandel's novels fall into the category of mystery and science fiction. How
would you relate mystery fiction with science technology?

. . . .

. . . .

question 29

Mandel novels generally have a broad cast of characters. In your opinion how
complicated it is for the author to manage such a cast of characters?

. . . .

. . . .

question 30

Mandel's fourth book, *Station Eleven,* has been a huge hit. How would you distinguish *Station Eleven* from her other novels?

. . . .

question 31

Jeevan, a paramedic in training, tries to save Arthur by giving him CPR, but he couldn't save him. In your opinion, how different would the story have been if Arthur was alive?

. . . .

question 32

In the end, Kristen leaves the traveling symphony towards the south. In your opinion, what could be their next destination?

. . . .

question 33

Kristen did not exactly remember the flu outbreak. If you were Kristen, would you want to be able to recall those memories? Why or why not?

· ·

question 34

Station Eleven is a post-apocalyptic tale. How do you think the story would
have gone if it was about the events that occurred before the flu outbreak?

· ·

. . . .

question 35

The novel explores the end of civilization after the catastrophe. How do you think the story would be different if the catastrophe were something other than the flu, such as war?

. . . .

. . . .

question 36

The novel is a complete blend of mystery, suspense, and history. If you had
the chance to rewrite this, how would you have ended the story?

. . . .

question 37

In *Station Eleven*, every character has its own plotline. If you had the chance to be a part of the story, which character would you choose and why?

. . . .

question 38

Clarke Thompson, Arthur's British friend, works as a curator at the Museum of Civilization. If you could donate something to the museum, what will you contribute?

. . . .

Quiz Questions

. . . .

question 39

_____ died on the same night as the Georgia flu outbreak in the city.

. . . .

question 40

"Survival is insufficient" is a famous line from _____.

question 41

True or false: Miranda was Arthur's fourth wife.

question 42

Kirsten leaves with the _____ for the south.

question 43

True or false: Clark Thompson was Arthur's American best friend.

. . . .

question 44

Tyler Leander grows up to be the religious leader known as
_____.

. . . .

question 45

Arthur was playing the role of _____.

question 46

True or false: Emily St. John Mandel is a Canadian novelist.

. . . .

question 47

Emily has written _____ novels so far.

question 48

Emily has won the National Book Award for _____.

question 49

True or false: *Station Eleven* has been translated into 12 languages.

. . . .

question 50

She has studied _____ at the School of Toronto Dance Theatre.

. . . .

Quiz Answers

1. Arthur
2. Star Trek
3. False; she was Arthur's first wife.
4. traveling symphony
5. False; he was Arthur's British friend.
6. prophet
7. King Lear
8. True
9. four
10. Station Eleven
11. False; it has been translated into 27 languages.
12. contemporary dance

THE END

Want to promote your book group? Register here.

FREE Download: Bonus Books Included
*Claim Yours with **Any Purchase** of* Conversation Starters!

  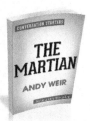

How to claim your free download:

7. <u>LEAVE MY AMAZON REVIEW.</u>
You Can Also Use "Write a Customer Review" Button

8. <u>ENTER YOUR BEST EMAIL HERE.</u>
NO SPAM. Your Email is Never Shared and is Protected

Or Scan Above

9. **RECEIVE YOUR FREE DOWNLOAD.**
Download is Instantly Delivered to Inbox